LET'S DRAW STEP BY STEP

Let's Draw with CHALK

KASIA DUDZIUK

WINDMILL BOOKS

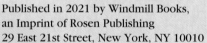

Published in 2021 by Windmill Books,
an Imprint of Rosen Publishing
29 East 21st Street, New York, NY 10010

Copyright © Arcturus Holdings Ltd, 2021

Cataloging-in-Publication Data

Names: Dudziuk, Kasia.
Title: Let's draw with chalk / Kasia Dudziuk.
Description: New York : Windmill Books, 2021. | Series: Let's draw step by step | Includes glossary and index.
Identifiers: ISBN 9781499485097 (pbk.) | ISBN 9781499485110 (library bound) | ISBN 9781499485103 (6 pack) | ISBN 9781499485127 (ebook)
Subjects: LCSH: Chalk drawing--Juvenile literature. | Drawing--Technique--Juvenile literature.
Classification: LCC NC867.D839 2021 | DDC 741.2'3--dc23

Manufactured in the United States of America

CPSIA Compliance Information: Batch BS20WM: For Further Information contact Rosen Publishing, New York, New York at 1-800-237-9932

Contents

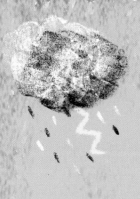

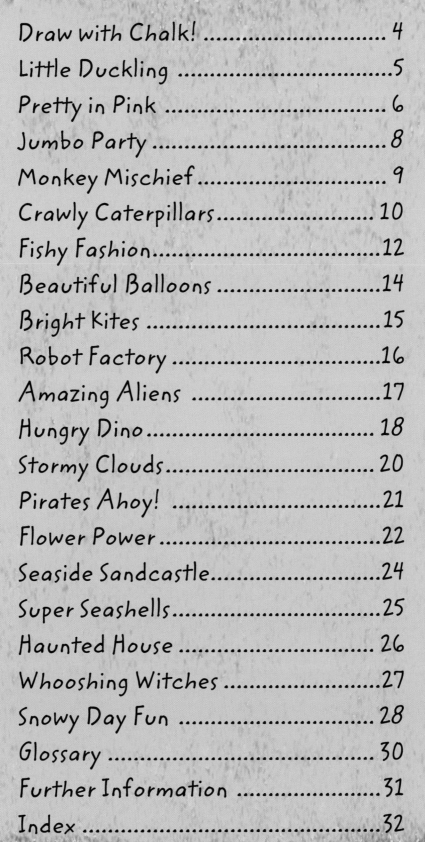

DRAW WITH CHALK!

In this book you'll learn how to create lots of fun pictures—all with chalk! Below are the different ways that chalk is used in this book. If you're not sure how an effect is created, just come back to this page to find out.

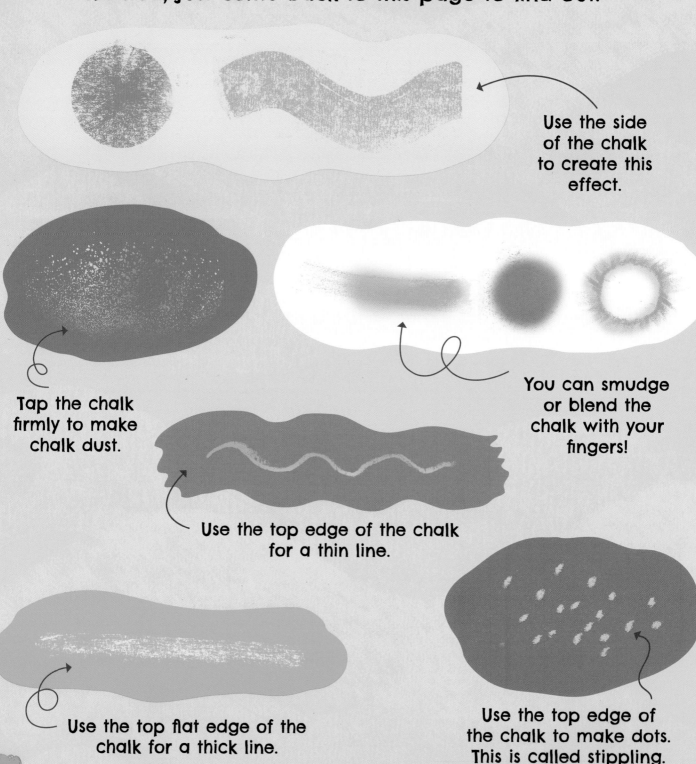

Use the side of the chalk to create this effect.

Tap the chalk firmly to make chalk dust.

You can smudge or blend the chalk with your fingers!

Use the top edge of the chalk for a thin line.

Use the top flat edge of the chalk for a thick line.

Use the top edge of the chalk to make dots. This is called stippling.

LITTLE DUCKLING

Draw simple orange outlines, then fill with yellow strokes.
Add ripples or splashes on the pond with white chalk.

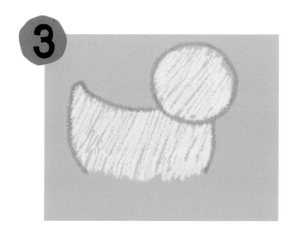

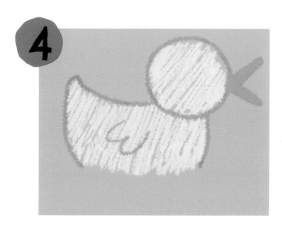

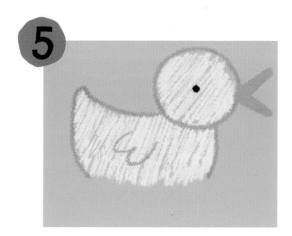

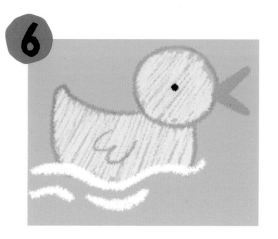

PRETTY IN PINK

Start with bold pink shapes, then add details in black with the top edge of the chalk.

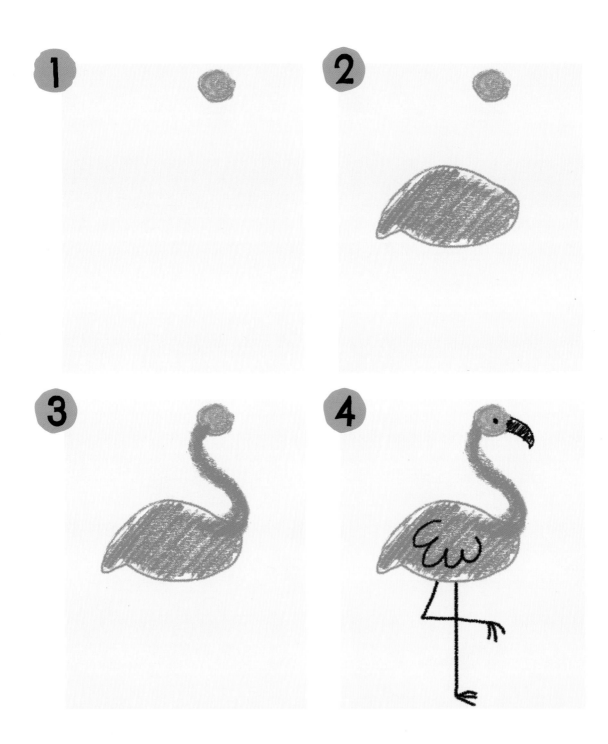

Flamingos are pink because of the food they eat.

Chicks are born gray and turn pink after two years.

Use the sides of white and pink chalk to add reflections.

JUMBO PARTY

Create patterns using spots, stripes,
or shapes in different chalks.

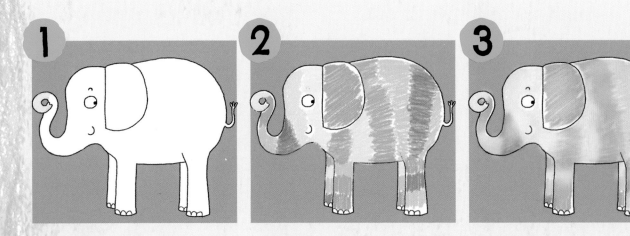

MONKEY MISCHIEF

Layer black and orange chalks, then
blend with your fingers.

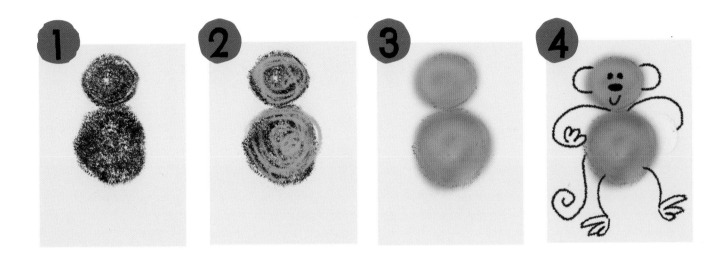

Can you make this swinging monkey?

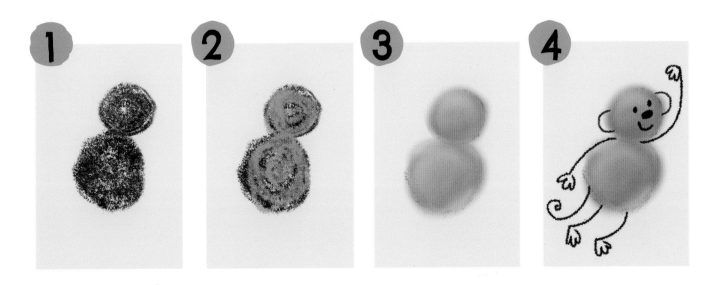

CRAWLY CATERPILLARS

Use the ends of your chalks, twisting to create circles. Then add legs and faces.

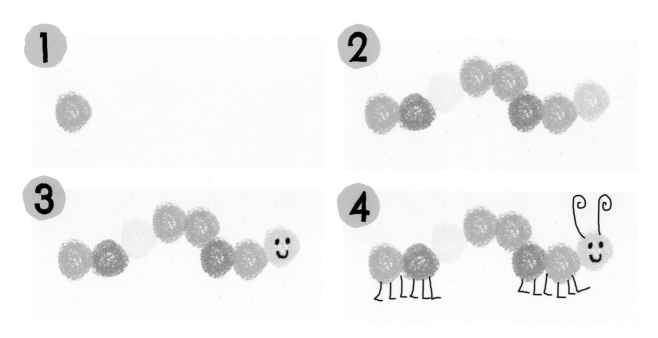

Or layer two chalks, smudging upward to make a hairy caterpillar!

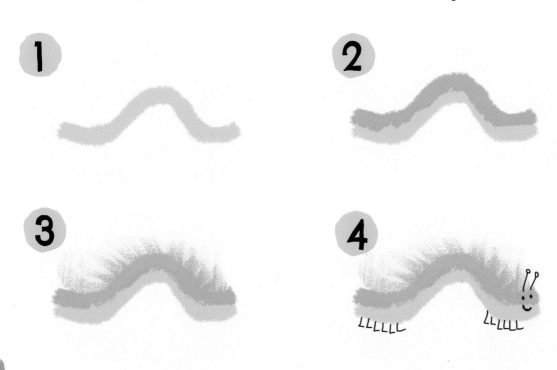

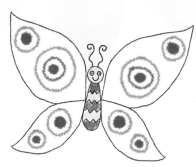

Caterpillars love to munch on leaves.

When they have eaten enough,
they build a snug home around
themselves called a cocoon.

Inside the cocoon, the
caterpillar changes
into a beautiful butterfly!

FISHY FASHION

Use different chalks to add patterns to your fish.
Smudge, blend—get creative!

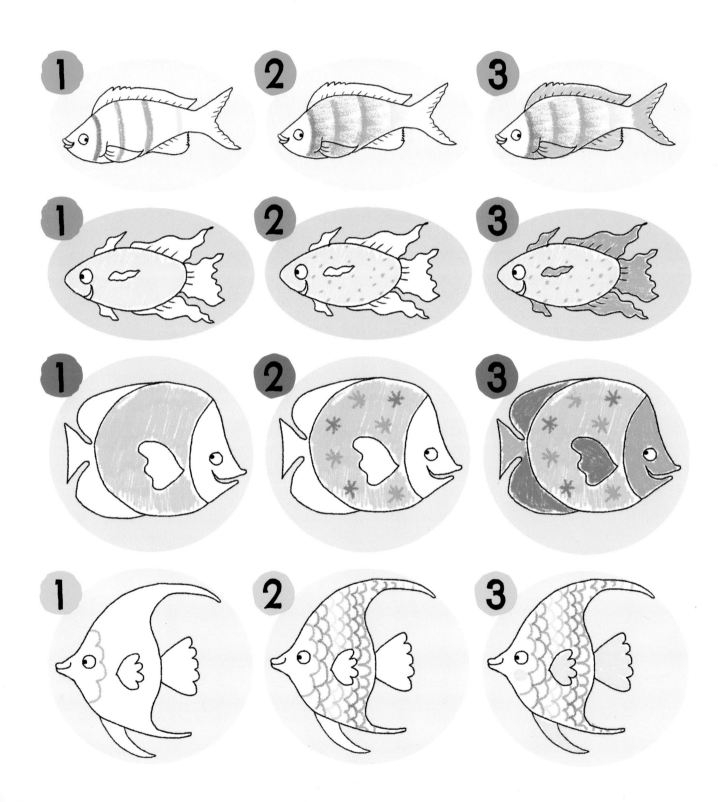

Dolphins live in family groups called pods.

The smallest seahorse is the size of a grain of rice!

Jellyfish live in oceans all over the world.

Coral reefs are home to many sea creatures, such as fish, sharks, rays, sponges, starfish, and many more!

BEAUTIFUL BALLOONS

Use bold stripes to make your balloon.
Add a basket and ropes—ready to fly!

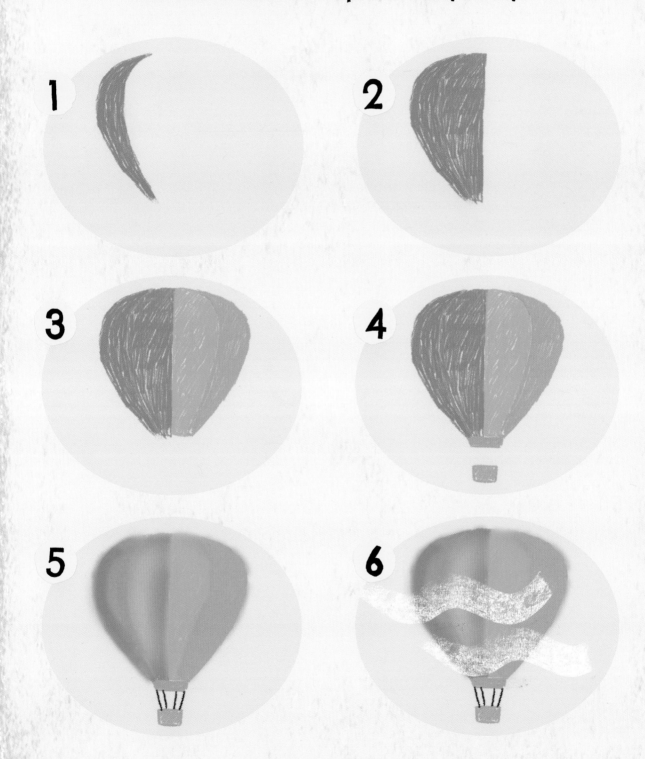

BRIGHT KITES

Shade in triangles and squares with different chalks to create cool kites.

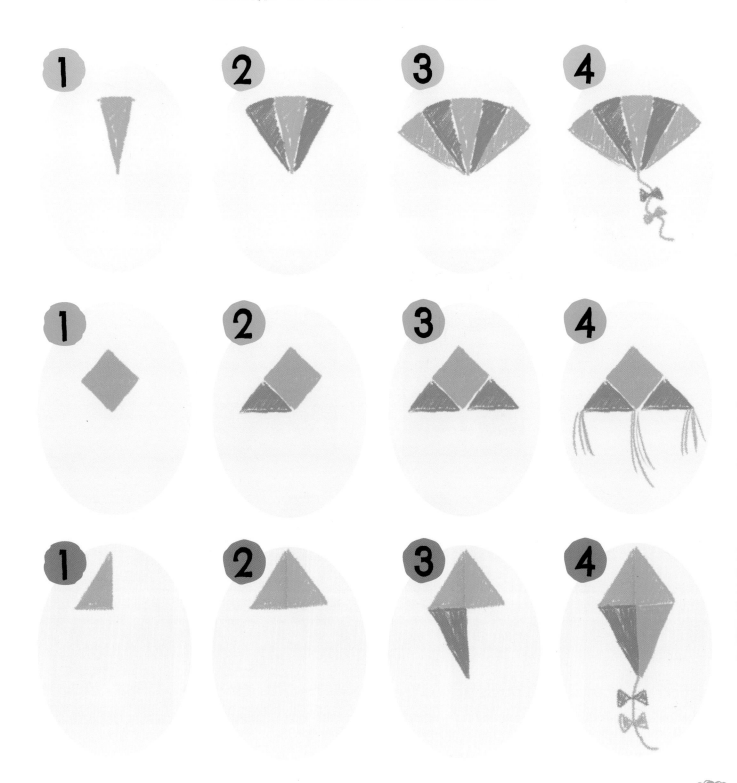

ROBOT FACTORY

Use two rectangles or circles to create
these awesome robots.

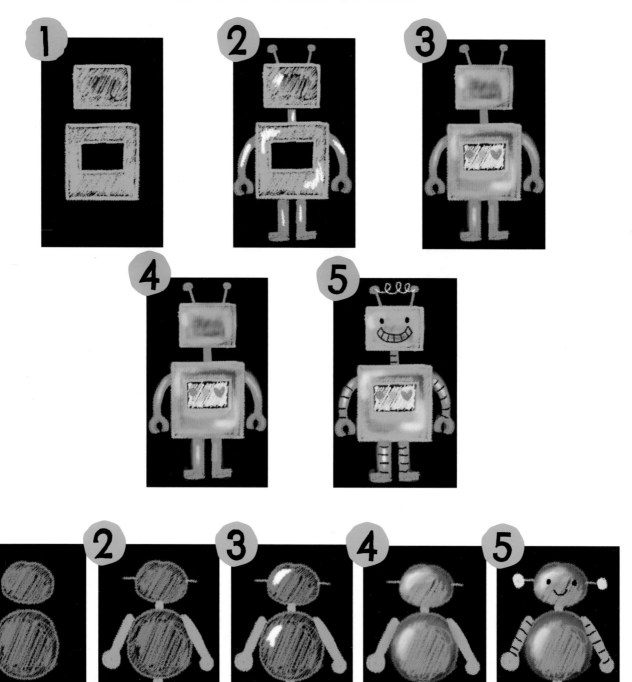

Add white over your chalk shading and smudge
to create a metallic effect.

AMAZING ALIENS

Draw outlines, then decorate your aliens
with spots, stripes, or blended chalks.

1

2

3

1

2

3

1

2

3

HUNGRY DINO

Draw oval shapes for the body and head.
Shade in stripes and blend up for the neck.

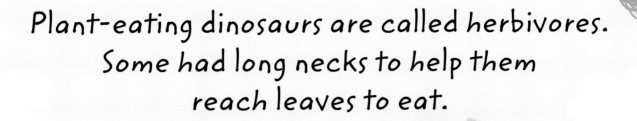

Plant-eating dinosaurs are called herbivores.
Some had long necks to help them
reach leaves to eat.

Stegosaurus (STEG-oh-SORE-us)
had bony plates on its back to
protect it from predators.

Meat-eating dinosaurs
are called carnivores.

STORMY CLOUDS

Layer black and white chalk to make dark clouds.
Add dashes for rain and bold yellow zigzags for lightning!

1

2

3

4

PIRATES AHOY!

Follow these steps to create a pirate captain
and first mate for your ship.

FLOWER POWER

Draw, layer, and blend different chalks to
create bright flowers.

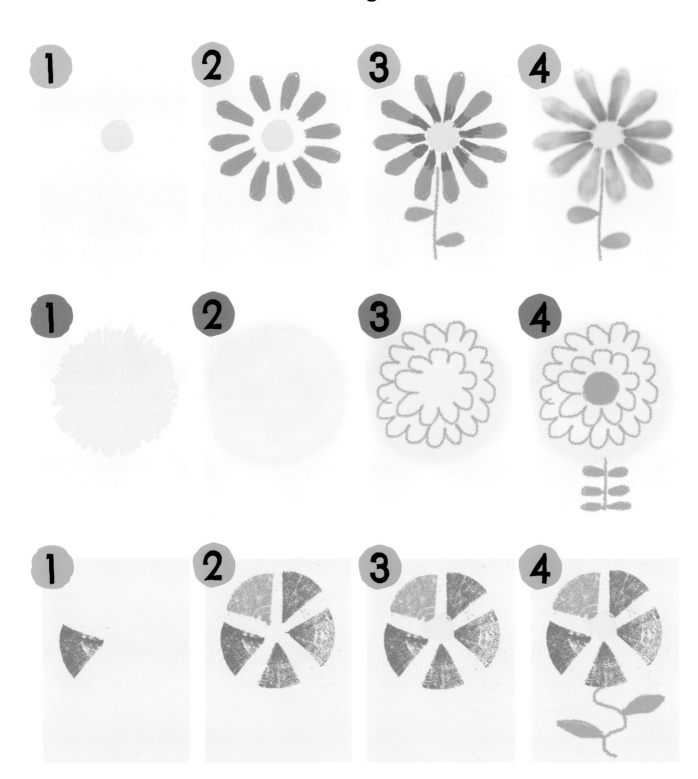

Busy bees travel from flower to flower.
They collect nectar and spread pollen.

Bees communicate
by dancing!

One bee will do a
waggle-dance to tell
other bees where the
best flowers are.

SEASIDE SANDCASTLE

Use the sides of your chalks to create shapes for an eye-catching castle.

1

2

3

4

5

6

SUPER SEASHELLS

Draw a simple outline, then decorate
with shading and blending.

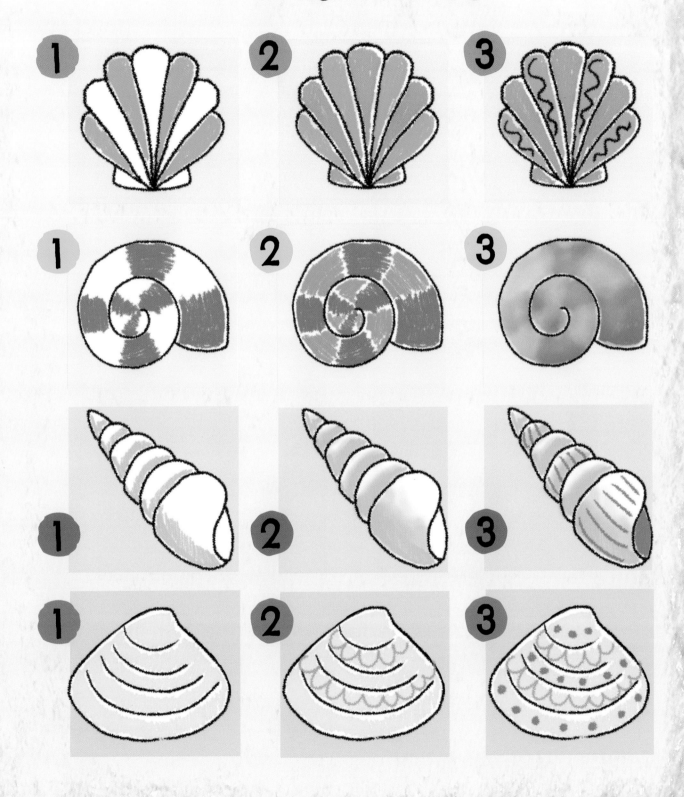

HAUNTED HOUSE

Use the side of white chalk to create spooky shapes.
Then add ghostly details!

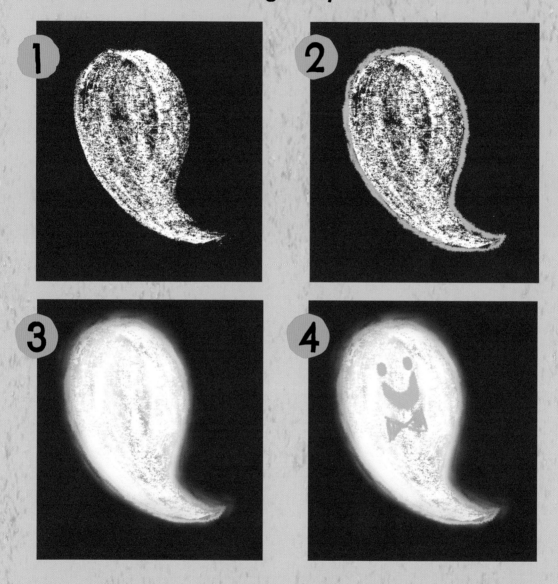

Eeek! Black chalk is perfect for making bat shapes.

WHOOSHING WITCHES

Start with a broom, then build up the witch to ride it.
Smudge the end of the broomstick to give it
some high-speed power!

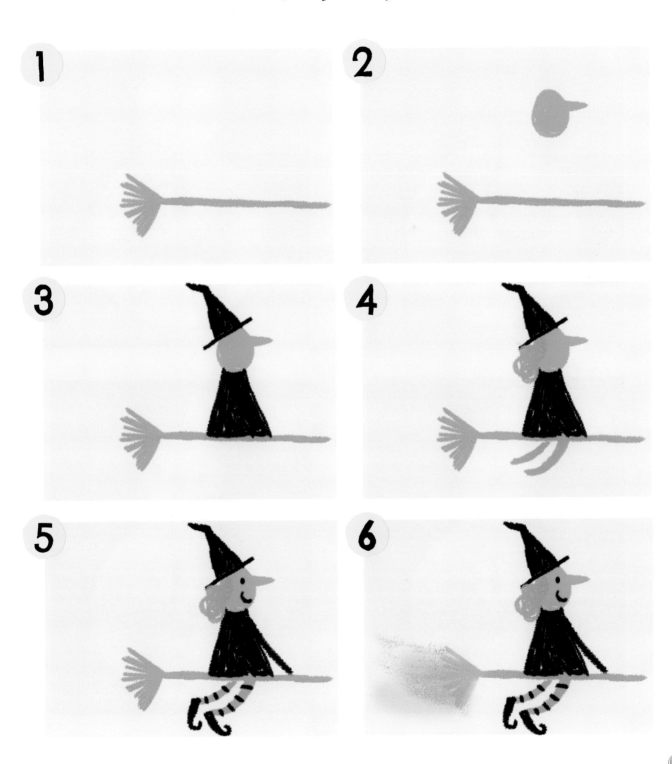

SNOWY DAY FUN

Spin white chalk around on its side to create
a snowman. Then dress him up!

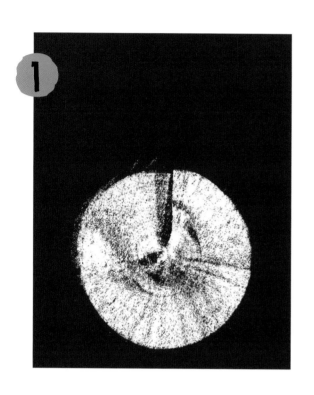

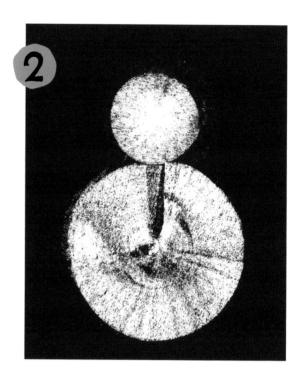

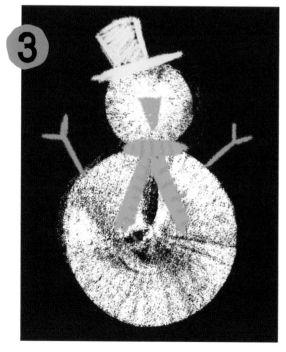

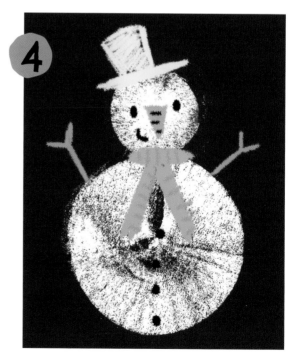

When the weather turns cold, it's time to dress up warm.

Many animals live in cold places. Reindeer, or caribou, have to dig through the snow in winter to find food.

Penguins are birds that cannot fly. Most live in cold, icy Antarctica.

Glossary

blend To rub or mix two or more colors together.

cocoon A silky case that a caterpillar spins around itself.

coral reef A ridge of rock in the sea where corals grow.

metallic Having the look and color of metal.

outline A simple line to show the shape of an object.

predator An animal that catches and kills other animals
for food.

reflection When one surface throws back the light before it, causing
a mirror image of the object in the surface.

snowflake A single flake of snow.

sponge A small sea creature that has a body with many holes.

Remember that you can
turn back to page 4 to check how
to create any of the effects
used in this book!

Further Information

Books to read

Get Into: Drawing by Kate Rochester, Wayland, 2017

How to Draw Amazing Animals and Incredible Insects
by Fiona Gowen, Barron's Educational Series, 2015

Let's Make Art series by Susie Brooks, Wayland, 2019

Step-by-Step Drawing Book by Fiona Watt, Usborne Publishing, 2014

The Beginner Art Book for Kids by Korri Freeman,
Rockridge Press, 2019

Websites

http://aminahsworld.org
You can create your own art at Aminah's World, from the Columbus
Museum of Art.

http://bomomo.com
Create some amazing patterns with bomomo!

www.tate.org.uk/kids
There's lots to discover at the Tate Kids website, with information about
artists and lots of ideas to try.

http://toytheater.com/category/art
There are lots of activities to try at Toy Theater, including doodles with
animals, artists, and the alphabet.

Publisher's note to educators and parents: Our editors have carefully reviewed these websites to
ensure that they are suitable for students. Many websites change frequently, however, and we cannot
guarantee that a site's future contents will continue to meet our high standards of quality and educational
value. Be advised that students should be closely supervised whenever they access the Internet.

Index

A
air balloon 14
aliens 17

B
bat 26
bees 23
butterflies 11, 23

C
caterpillars 10, 11
clouds 20, 29
coral reef 13

D
dinosaurs 18, 19
dolphins 13
duckling 5

E
effects 4
elephants 8

F
fish 12, 13
flamingos 6-7
flowers 22, 23

G
ghost 26

J
jellyfish 13

K
kites 15

L
leaves 11, 19

M
monkeys 9

O
ocean 13

P
penguins 29
pirates 21

R
reflections 7
reindeer 29
robots 16

S
sandcastle 24
seahorse 13
seashells 25
snail 23
snow 28, 29
snowman 28, 29

T
trees 19, 29

W
water 5, 7, 13, 20
witch 27